GOOD TO BE GREEN

Garbage or Recyling?

Written by DEBORAH CHANCELLOR

Illustrated by DIANE EWEN

CRABTREE
PUBLISHING COMPANY
WWW.CRABTREEBOOKS.COM

Before, During, and After Reading Prompts

Activate Prior Knowledge and Make Predictions
Read the title of the book to the children and look at the illustrations. Ask children what they think the book may be about. Ask them questions related to the title, such as:
- What does "recycle" mean?
- Can you name some items you recycled today? How about items you threw into the garbage?

During Reading
Stop at various points during reading and ask children questions related to the story:
- What do Nasir and Nadia use to make their robot? *(see pages 8–9)*
- How do Nasir and Nadia sort their garbage? *(see pages 10–11)*
- Why do Nasir, Nadia, and Dad go to the landfill and the recycling depot? *(see pages 12–15)*
- What kind of garbage do Nasir, Nadia, and Dad take with them? *(see pages 14–15)*

- What do Nasir and Nadia learn about recycling? *(see pages 18–21)*

After Reading
Look at the information panels, then talk together about recycling. Ask children the following prompting questions:
- What kind of materials can be recycled? *(see pages 9, 11)*
- What happens to garbage that is not recycled? *(see pages 18–19)*
- Why is plastic bad for the planet? *(see page 15)*
- How can we reduce the amount of plastic we use? *(see pages 20–21)*
- What types of objects can we reuse? Why is it good to reuse things? *(see page 25)*

Do the Quiz together *(see pages 28–29)*. Refer back to the information panels to find answers.

Crabtree Publishing Company

www.crabtreebooks.com   1-800-387-7650

Published in Canada
Crabtree Publishing
616 Welland Ave.
St. Catharines, Ontario
L2M 5V6

Published in the United States
Crabtree Publishing
PMB 59051
350 Fifth Avenue, 59th Floor
New York, New York 10118

PUBLISHED IN 2020 BY CRABTREE PUBLISHING COMPANY

First published in 2019 by Wayland (an imprint of Hachette Children's Group, part of Hodder and Stoughton)
Copyright © Hodder and Stoughton, 2019

Author: Deborah Chancellor
Illustrator: Diane Ewen
Editorial Director: Kathy Middleton
Editors: Sarah Peutrill, Ellen Rodger
Designer: Cathryn Gilbert
Print and production coordinator: Katherine Berti

Printed in the U.S.A./122019/CG20191101

Library and Archives Canada Cataloguing in Publication

Title: Garbage or recycling / written by Deborah Chancellor ; illustrated by Diane Ewen.
Other titles: Rubbish or recycling
Names: Chancellor, Deborah, author. | Ewen, Diane (Illustrator), illustrator.
Description: Series statement: Good to be green | Previously published under title: Rubbish or recycling. London: Wayland, 2019. | Includes index. | "A story about garbage and why it's important to recycle".
Identifiers: Canadiana (print) 20190194308 | Canadiana (ebook) 20190194316 | ISBN 9780778772828 (hardcover) | ISBN 9780778772897 (softcover) | ISBN 9781427124708 (HTML)
Subjects: LCSH: Recycling (Waste, etc.)—Juvenile literature. | LCSH: Refuse and refuse disposal—Juvenile literature. | LCSH: Sustainable living—Juvenile literature. | LCSH: Environmentalism— Juvenile literature.
Classification: LCC TD794.5 .C53 2020 | DDC j363.72/82—dc23

Library of Congress Cataloging-in-Publication Data

Names: Chancellor, Deborah, author. | Ewen, Diane (Illustrator), illustrator.
Title: Garbage or recycling? / written by Deborah Chancellor ; illustrated by Diane Ewen.
Description: New York : Crabtree Publishing Company, [2020] | Series: Good to be green | Includes index.
Identifiers: LCCN 2019043890 (print) | LCCN 2019043891 (ebook) | ISBN 9780778772828 (hardcover) | ISBN 9780778772897 (paperback) | ISBN 9781427124708 (ebook)
Subjects: LCSH: Refuse and refuse disposal--Juvenile literature. | Recycling (Waste, etc.)--Juvenile literature.
Classification: LCC TD792 .C536 2020 (print) | LCC TD792 (ebook) | DDC 628.4/4--dc23
LC record available at https://lccn.loc.gov/2019043890
LC ebook record available at https://lccn.loc.gov/2019043891

Garbage or Recyling?

A story about garbage and why it's important to recycle

It was a rainy
weekend.
Nasir and Nadia
were bored.

But then Nadia
had a **brainwave**.
"Let's make a model
out of junk!" she said.

School Recycling
Competition

Make a JUNK MODEL
from
RECYCLING
Win a Trophy!

6

"Should we make a robot?" asked Nasir.
"Great idea!" said Nadia. "We can enter it
into the school competition."

"We need to use things that can be **recycled**," said Nadia. She picked a can out of the recycling box.

"We can call our model a recycling robot."

Cans made from a metal called **aluminum** can be recycled to make new cans, or used to make parts for planes and bikes.

Nasir and Nadia made a pile of things that can be recycled, and a pile of things that can't.

We need to sort our **garbage**. Over half of the trash that ends up in our garbage cans could be recycled instead. We can recycle paper, cardboard, glass, most metals, and some kinds of plastic.

"Look at all this plastic!" said Nasir.
"It's a shame we can't recycle it,"
said Nadia.

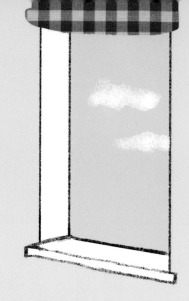

Dad came into the kitchen. "What a mess!" he said.

"We need to go to the **landfill** and the **recycling depot**," said Dad. The twins helped carry all the plastic to the car.

Plastic garbage can be harmful to **wildlife**. Sadly, a lot of it ends up in the ocean. We all need to use less plastic to stop this from happening.

The twins were shocked
by what they saw
at the depot.

Garden
Waste

Paper and
Cardboard

"Look at all this **waste**!" said Nasir.

"Can any of it be recycled?" asked Nadia.

"Some of it can," said Dad.

Household
Waste

"What about the rest?" asked Nasir.
"It will be buried at the landfill site,"
said Dad.

When **plastic** is thrown out, it takes a long time to break down into safe, natural materials. Some plastic bottles take 500 years to do this.

The twins didn't like this idea very much.

"We must recycle as much as we can," said Nadia.

"And **reuse** what we can't recycle," said Nasir.

We need to **reuse** things instead of throwing them away. Don't throw out your old toys— share them with someone else instead!

Back at home, Nasir and Nadia began building their junk model.

The twins worked very hard
and the day flew by in a flash.

"Look at our recycling
robot!" said Nadia.
"Wow!" said Dad.
"It's amazing!"

Reuse things made from glass, metal, and plastic. Reusing items saves the **energy** it would take to recycle them or make replacements.

The twins couldn't wait to take their junk model to school. They entered the competition and won first prize!

The recycling robot helped everyone
sort out recycling from garbage.

Garbage

Early Morning

Recycling

Quiz time

Which of these things are true? Read the book again to find out!

(Cover up the answers on page 29.)

1. It's impossible to recycle a soda or juice can.

2. Over half of the garbage we throw out could be recycled instead.

3. Plastic garbage often ends up in the sea.

4. Plastic bottles can take up to five years to break down into safe materials.

5. We can't reuse things made of glass.

Answers

1. **False**

Aluminum cans are recycled to make parts for planes and bikes. *(See page 9)*

2. **True**

We need to sort our trash more carefully. *(See page 11)*

3. **True**

Lots of plastic waste ends up in the sea and is harmful to sea life. *(See page 15)*

4. **False**

Plastic bottles can take up to 500 years to break down. *(See page 19)*

5. **False**

Glass can be reused. This saves the energy it takes to make new glass. *(See page 25)*

Get active

In the story, Nasir and Nadia use recycled trash to make a junk model of a robot. Think of some other models you could make with recycled trash, such as a space ship or a time machine. Then collect and sort some garbage for recycling, to make a model of your own.

Collect some materials that can be recycled, and some that can't. Use scraps of these materials to make a collage all about recycling.

Try to find out about sea animals and birds that are in danger because of plastic pollution, for example the green turtle and the albatross. Ask an adult to help you find out more. You could watch a TV documentary, read a book, or look at an environment website together.

Make a short film about plastic pollution in the oceans. You could use the video camera on a smartphone to do this. Think carefully about what you want to say before you begin and make a simple storyboard (a series of drawings showing each scene) before you start filming. You could include photos of endangered sea creatures and plastic garbage that has been washed up on beaches.

A note about sharing this book

The *Good to Be Green* series provides a starting point for further discussion on important environmental issues, such as pollution, climate change, and endangered wildlife. Each topic is relevant to both children and adults.

Garbage or Recycling?

This story explores some issues surrounding recycling. *Garbage or Recycling?* demonstrates key concepts about recycling, such as the need to sort our household waste carefully. It also includes the idea of reusing everyday items, to save the energy it takes to make replacements. The story and the nonfiction elements in *Garbage or Recycling?* encourage the reader to conclude that we all need to reuse and recycle more often, because it is good for the environment and helps to save endangered wildlife.

How to use the book

This book can be shared with children individually or in small and large groups. It can also be used as a starting point for discussion about food waste. Clear illustrations support the story to raise confidence in children who are starting to read on their own.

The story introduces vocabulary relevant to the theme of recycling, such as: *waste, garbage or trash, recycling, reuse, landfill site, glass, metal, plastic*, and *aluminum*. Some of the vocabulary in the story and information panels will be unfamiliar to the reader. These words are in bold text, and they are defined in the glossary on page 32. When reading the story for the first time, refer to the glossary with the children.

There is also an index on page 32. Encourage children to use the index when you are talking about the book. For example, ask them to use the index to find the page that mentions wildlife (page 15). It is important that children know that information can be found in books as well as searched for on the Internet with a responsible adult.

Glossary

aluminum A metal that can be recycled (made into something new)

brainwave A sudden idea

energy Power that is used to make something work, such as electricity

garbage Things you don't want anymore that cannot be recycled or reused

landfill A place where garbage is buried in the ground

plastic A machine-made material that can be molded into any shape

recycled When trash is changed into something useful

recycling depot A place where materials that can be recycled are sorted

reuse To use something again

waste Things that are not wanted, or can't be used again

wildlife Animals that are not tame and live in their natural habitat

Index